ice cream
and frozen desserts

TRIDENT
PRESS
INTERNATIONAL

Published by:
TRIDENT PRESS INTERNATIONAL
801 12th Avenue South
Suite 302
Naples, FL 34102 U.S.A.
(c)Trident Press
Tel: (941) 649 7077
Fax: (941) 649 5832
Email: tridentpress@worldnet.att.net
Website: www.trident-international.com

acknowledgements

Ice cream and frozen desserts
Packaged by R&R Publications Marketing Pty Ltd
Creative Director: Paul Sims
Production Manager: Anthony Carroll

Food Photography: William Meppem,
Quentin Bacon, John Street, Paul Austin

Food Stylists: Elise Pascoe,
Anne Fayle, Donna Hay

Recipe Development: Elise Pascoe,
Merl Kershaw, Donna Hay

Proof Reader: Andrea Tarttelin

Includes Index
ISBN 1 582 79119 8
EAN 9 781582 791197

First Edition Printed September 2000
Computer Typeset in Humanist 521
& Times New Roman

Printed by APP Printing, Singapore
Film Scanning by Color Gallery, Malaysia

contents

introduction

Who Invented Ice Cream?

A popular legend attributes the invention of ice cream to the Roman emperor Nero, who in the first century A.D. sent runners to fetch snow from the top of nearby mountains and then had it flavoured with wine and fruit juices. In truth, historical records suggest that ice cream originated much earlier. There is evidence that the ancient Chinese were already making water ices at the beginning of recorded history, and they were probably doing so well before. From China frozen desserts spread to Arabia, India and Persia.

Marco Polo encountered flavoured ices on his journeys to the East and was responsible for introducing them to Italy. The dessert he introduced was probably the forerunner of what we would call a milk ice (rather than a water ice, or sherbet), goat's milk probably having been added to the original Chinese water ices by the Arabians. The art of making frozen desserts in Italy was refined with the discovery of salt as an aid to freezing. Ice cream (along with another Italian innovation, the dinner fork) was introduced to France in the sixteenth century by Catherine de Medici. From there it quickly spread to England and then to the rest of Europe.

The dessert we now know as ice cream - at first called cream ice - was introduced by a French chef to King Charles I of England early in the seventeenth century. Initially it was available only to royalty and court nobility, but by the end of the seventeenth century, commoners too were indulging in frozen desserts. By 1676 there were 250 shops selling ice cream and ices in Paris alone, and the French government gave ice cream vendors official status as a trade guild. Despite the rapid spread of ices and ice cream throughout Europe, the enormous and widespread popularity that ice cream enjoys today is a relatively modern, and largely American, phenomenon, attributable in no small way to the development of reliable refrigeration in the twentieth century. The familiar hand-cranked ice cream churn was invented in 1846 by an American woman named Nancy Johnson (about whom little else is known). The first ice cream cone evidently was sold at the St. Louis World Exposition of 1904, when an ice cream vendor ran out of dishes and started substituting rolled-up wafers from a neighbouring concessionaire. During the 1920s a variety of frozen desserts were invented in rapid succession, including the Eskimo pie, the Good Humour bar, and the Popsicle. In 1939 a machine for making soft ice cream, by incorporating a great deal of air into the mixture, was perfected and fast-food businesses serving ice cream or ice milk quickly proliferated. Unfortunately, as the manufacture of ice cream became big business in the United States, quality often suffered. Gelatin and milk were introduced into sherbets; flour and whole eggs were added to ice cream, and the amount of fresh cream was drastically reduced.

Today ice cream and frozen desserts continue to gain in popularity, and many commercial manufacturers are returning to stricter quality standards. A new generation of home ice cream freezers - smaller, easier to use, and more efficient than earlier versions - are inspiring ice cream enthusiasts to make homemade frozen desserts on a regular basis, not just for the occasional special party. Thousands of electric ice cream machines and pre-chilled canisters now stand ready to swing into action at a moment's notice.

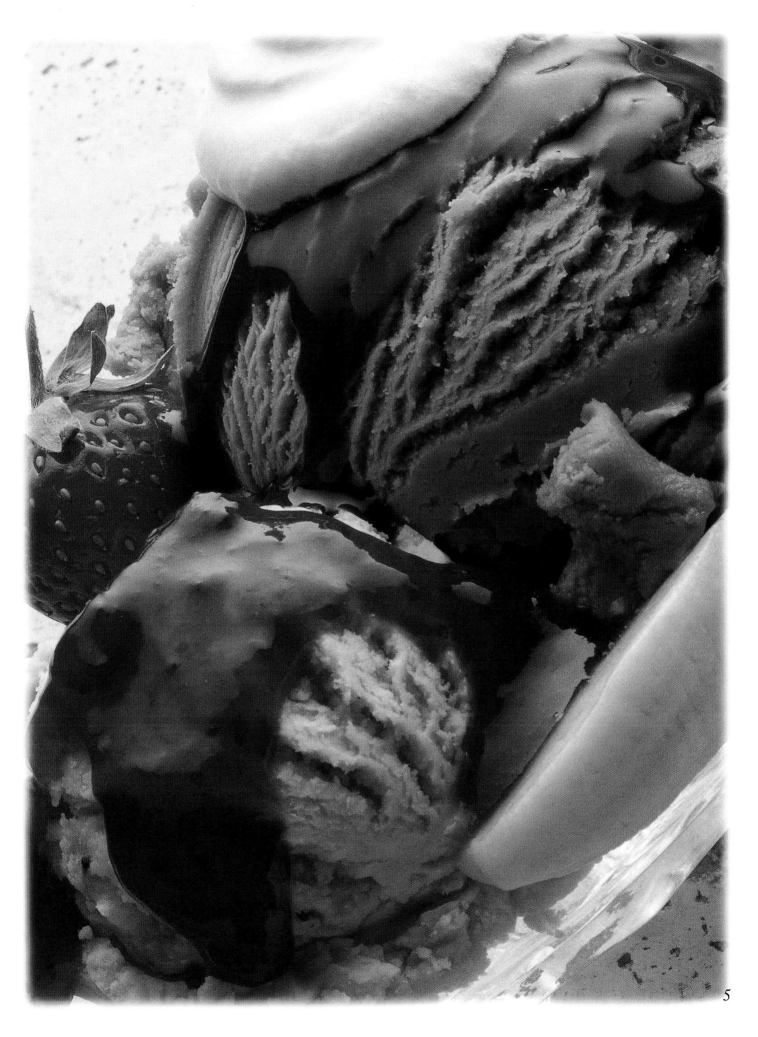

basic
knowledge

Sweet Freeze: A Primer

From icy poles to Peach Melba, frozen specialties run the gamut from simple to sophisticated. Gelato, glace, ice cream, nieve, granita, helado, ice milk, sherbet, sorbet, sorbetto, frozen yoghurt, water ice - names and distinctions for these icy delights blur across cultural boundaries, reflecting their enormous popularity worldwide. Here are some broad definitions to help sort it all out:

Ice Cream

Made from either a cooked custard or uncooked base. Ice cream made with eggs and cream is higher in fat than ice "cream" made with skim milk (low-fat or nonfat). As a rule, the higher the fat content of the base mixture, the creamier the texture; incorporating gelatin, egg substitutes, or lecithin (an emulsifier made from soybeans) into mixtures made with skim milk makes the texture creamier.

Granita

A type of water ice (sherbet) with a slightly grainy texture, the result of freezing without constant churning. Granita is traditionally served slightly thawed and slushy, but if you like a smoother texture similar to a churn-frozen sherbet, purée it in a food processor shortly before serving.

Ice

A generic term for a sherbet, milk ice is sherbet to which a small amount of milk or cream has been added.

Sorbet, Sherbet and Sorbetto

A water ice usually made with fruit (or fruit juice) and sugar syrup. Other names for this product include ice, water ice, Italian ice, and fruit ice. To further complicate the issue, sometimes "sherbet" is the name for milk ice; "sorbet" is water ice. A small serving of wine - or citrus-flavoured sorbet - a palate cleanser - is sometimes served between courses to freshen the taste buds.

Frozen yoghurt

Has a smooth texture similar to ice cream and a slightly acidic taste that complements fruit particularly well.

Dream Machines

For anyone who loves frozen desserts, the new generation of ice cream freezers is pure dreamery, making it easier than ever before to enjoy your favourite frozen specialties at home anytime you like, not just on special occasions. Compact, convenient, and highly efficient, these machines stand ready to crank out icy pleasures at a moment's notice.

Although a few recipes in this book are made by still-freezing the base mixture in the freezer compartment of a refrigerator, most employ churn-freezing, using one of the following types of hand or electric-powered ice cream makers:

Salt and Ice Bucket Freezer

Licking the dasher after hand cranking the ice cream churn is a sweet childhood memory for many ice cream enthusiasts. This type of machine features a bucket fitted with a lidded metal canister that holds the base mixture. Powered by a hand crank or electric motor, the canister rotates continuously, surrounded by ice and rock salt, causing the contents of the canister to freeze as it is churned by a stationary dasher. This machine requires about 20-30 minutes of cranking for each batch. The slower the freezing process, the finer the texture while fast freezing yields an icy, coarse texture. One variation on this type of machine needs no salt or ice because it operates inside the freezer compartment of a refrigerator, with the power cord snaking out through the closed door.

Prechilled Canister Freezer

This type of machine features a coolant sealed in a hollow metal canister. After the canister has chilled in the freezer compartment of a refrigerator for at least 8 hours, the base mixture is poured into the center of the canister, and the dasher assembly and lid are fitted into place. Hand-powered models have a crank that is rotated every 2 or 3 minutes until the mixture freezes (usually in about 15 minutes). Electric models require about the same amount of time.

Self-Contained Refrigerated Freezer

The Maserati of ice cream makers, this Italian design boasts a countertop unit with built-in refrigeration and motorized dasher. It is the easiest to use (and the most expensive), producing the smoothest texture of any machine for home use.

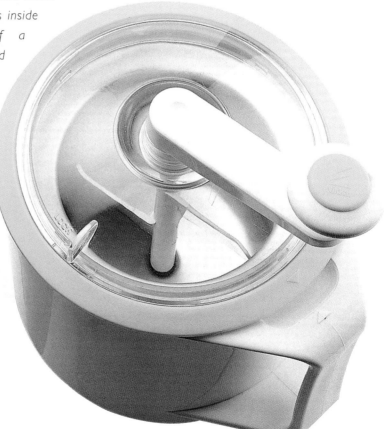

basic
ingredients

For ice cream to have a smooth, creamy texture, both the water molecules and the fat globules in the mixture must be suspended evenly, so that the ice crystals that form during freezing are very small. The basic ice cream ingredients, in addition to contributing flavour, help that to happen.

Many commercial ice cream manufacturers use emulsifiers and stabilizers to improve the texture of their product, mask or compensate for inferior ingredients or achieve an extended shelf life. Such artificial ingredients are never needed in ice cream made in small quantities at home with fresh, wholesome ingredients. There are also homemade ice cream recipes that call for such ingredients as cornstarch, instant vanilla pudding, gelatin, and flour in an attempt to simulate the texture produced by more expensive ingredients. Anyone who has tasted good homemade ice cream, made with pure, high quality ingredients, will find it hard to offer such pseudo-flavours to family and guests.

Cream

The butterfat in cream is primarily responsible for providing the rich, smooth texture of ice cream. In general, the higher the proportion of butterfat, the richer and smoother the ice cream. However, resist the temptation to substitute whipping cream for the half and half or milk in an ice cream recipe. Too much cream greatly increases the chance of producing ice cream flecked with butter. As a general rule, do not exceed a ratio of 75 percent cream to 25 percent milk.

Eggs

Egg yolks are cooked to form the custard base used in many ice cream recipes. They act as emulsifiers; that is, they keep the fat globules in milk and cream from clumping together. Use large eggs for all the recipes in this book. Yolks are most easily separated from whites when eggs are cold, but egg whites at room temperature provide more volume when whisked. Egg whites may be frozen until needed, then thawed in the refrigerator.

Fruit

Most fruits used to flavour ice cream contain naturally occurring pectin and a certain amount of fiber. Both of these substances help to keep milk fat and water molecules in an even suspension as they freeze.

Milk

Milk fat forms small globules in the ice cream mixture that help to keep the water molecules dispersed. The emulsifying action of cooked egg yolks helps keep these small fat globules from clumping together as they are churned. If they do form clumps, they will produce butter.

Sugar

Water in which sugar has been dissolved has a freezing point below $0°C/32°F$. Because of the sugar present, not all the water in ice cream freezes. Sugar thus helps keep ice cream from becoming a solid block of ice.

nectarine sorbet

sorbets and sherbets

Let your taste buds delight in the flavour

of cool Nectarine Sorbet, Melon Sherbet or a Strawberry Ice. You can frolic guiltlessly through this chilly wonderland because the recipes in this section are not only sinfully delicious, they contain less than 1 gram of fat per serving.

melon
sherbet

Photograph opposite

melon sherbet

ingredients

1pt/600ml/20fl oz water
³/₄ cup/180g/6oz caster sugar
1 tablespoon lemon juice
1kg/2 lb honeydew melon or
rockmelon
grated orange rind
1 teaspoon ginger essence
2 egg whites
4 drops food colour (optional)

Method:

1 *Put water, sugar and lemon juice in a heavy based saucepan and heat gently until sugar has dissolved. Increase heat and cook rapidly fo 5 minutes. Allow to cool.*
2 *Scoop flesh from the melon, remove pips and using a food processor or blender, purée.*
3 *Stir into sugar syrup the orange rind and ginger essence.*
4 *Beat egg whites until soft peaks form and fold into melon mixture.*
5 *Pour into ice cream maker, add colour if desired. Churn approximately 30 minutes or until blades stop.*
Note: *This looks great served in tiny halved melon skins (that have been reserved) as individual serving portions.*
Makes approximately
4 cups/1 litre/1³/₄pints

strawberry
and rhubarb sorbet

Method:

1 *In a heavy based saucepan combine rhubarb and water. Bring to a boil over medium heat and simmer, covered, until rhubarb is tender (approximately 5 minutes). Stir in sugar until dissolved.*

2 *Using a food processor or blender, purée the rhubarb. Place into a bowl.*

3 *Purée strawberries and stir into rhubarb mixture.*

4 *Pour into ice cream maker and churn approximately 20 minutes or until blades stop.*

**Makes approximately
6cups/1 1/2 litres/2 1/2 pts**

ingredients

**4 cups/500g/1 lb fresh rhubarb, cut
into 2 1/2cm/1 in lengths
1/4 cup/60ml/2fl oz water
1 1/2 cups/375g/12 1/2oz sugar
2 punnets/500g/1 lb fresh strawberries**

kiwi
fruit sorbet

Method:

1 *Put the water, lemon juice and caster sugar into a heavy based saucepan. Heat gently until the sugar has dissolved. Increase the heat and cook rapidly for 5 minutes. Allow to cool.*

2 *Using a food processor or blender, purée the kiwifruit and stir into the sugar syrup.*

3 *Beat the egg whites to soft peaks and fold into the mixture.*

4 *Pour into ice cream maker and churn approximately 30 minutes or until blades stop.*

**Makes approximately 6 cups/
1 1/2 litres/2 1/2pts**

ingredients

**2 1/2cups/600ml/1 pt water
2 tablespoons lemon juice
100g/3oz caster sugar
8-10 kiwifruit, peeled
2 egg whites**

watermelon
sherbet

Method:

1 Sprinkle sugar and salt over melon chunks and mix well. Once the sugar has dissolved, taste melon for sweetness; add more sugar if desired.

2 Purée melon, any juice it has released and egg whites in a blender or food processor. Chill well. Transfer to an ice cream machine and freeze according to manufacturer's instructions.

Note: Any of your favourite melons can be substituted for watermelon in this recipe. Be sure to reserve any juice that is released when you cut the melon into chunks.

**Makes approximately
4 cups/900ml/8fl oz**

ingredients

1/4 **cup/60g/2oz sugar**
1/4 **teaspoon salt**
**900ml/1 quart chilled watermelon
chunks, seeds removed
(about one 2kg/4lb melon)**
2 egg whites

wine
sorbet

Method:

1 A day ahead, in a saucepan combine 1 cup/ 250mL/8fl oz water, sugar, and half the wine. Stir to dissolve sugar; bring to a boil. Reduce heat and simmer 3 minutes. Allow syrup to cool.

2 Add remaining wine to syrup. Pour into a shallow container and freeze overnight.

3 Two to four hours before serving remove frozen mixture from freezer. Transfer to a food processor and process until smooth, about 20-30 seconds. Return mixture to freezer container or individual serving glasses and freeze to set.

4 Remove sorbet from the freezer 5-10 minutes before serving to soften slightly.

Note: This delicate palate refresher can be made from just about any table wine except a really tannic red. You can also use a sweet wine, but reduce the sugar in the syrup by a tablespoon. Riesling or White Zinfandel would be good wines to start with, but feel free to experiment with various whites, roses and reds.

ingredients

1/2 **cup/125g/4oz sugar**
**1 cup/250ml/8fl oz dry or slightly
sweet table wine**

Alcohol affects the freezing process, so don't omit the step of boiling half the wine with the syrup one day before you plan to serve the sorbet. This procedure removes some, but not all, of the alcohol, giving the sorbet just the right texture and flavour. The sorbet does not keep well, as it tends to separate in the freezer.

**Make approximately
1 1/2 cups/375ml/12 1/2fl oz**

watermelon
and strawberry sorbet

Method:

1 *Combine water and sugar in a saucepan and bring to the boil. Remove from heat and allow to cool completely.*

2 *In a food processor or blender puree watermelon flesh and strawberries.*

3 *Mix puree into sugar mixture and freeze in a stainless steel bowl. Whisk from time to time during freezing to give a smooth even texture. To serve, spoon into elegant glasses and at the last minute pour a tablespoon of champagne into each glass.*

Serves 8

ingredients

**1 cup/250ml/8fl oz water
2 tablespoons caster sugar
300g/10oz watermelon, skinned, seeds removed and chopped
250g/8oz strawberries, hulled
3/4 cup/190ml/6fl oz dry champagne (optional)**

fresh
apple sorbet

ingredients

**6 small tart green apples,
cored and peeled
I cup/250ml/8fl oz simple sugar syrup
(see page 74)
I tablespoon lemon juice**

Method:

1 *Blend apples in a blender or food processor with syrup and lemon juice until completely smooth.*
2 *Transfer to an ice cream machine and freeze according to manufacturer's instructions.*
   Note: *The flavour of this sorbet will vary with the variety of apple you choose.*
   **Makes approximately
   4 cups/1 litre/1 ³/₄ pints**

ruby
grapefruit sorbet

Photograph opposite

ingredients

**I cup/250g/8oz sugar
I tablespoon finely grated ruby
grapefruit rind
4 cups/I litre/I ³/₄pt ruby red
grapefruit juice
¹/₂ cup/125ml/4fl oz champagne or
sparkling white wine**

Method:

1 *Place sugar, grapefruit rind and 1 cup/250ml/ 8fl oz juice in a non-reactive saucepan and cook, stirring, over a low heat until sugar dissolves.*
2 *Combine sugar syrup, wine and remaining juice, pour into an ice cream maker and freeze following manufacturer's instructions. Alternately, pour mixture into a shallow freezerproof container and freeze until ice crystals start to form around the edges. Using a fork, stir to break up ice crystals. Repeat the process once more then freeze until firm.*
   Note: *Serve sorbet in scoops with slices of peach or nectarine. For this recipe, Ocean Spray ruby red grapefruit juice was used. It is available from supermarkets.*
   Serves 8

lemon
sherbet

ingredients

2¹/₂ cups/625g/1¹/₄lb sugar
3 cups/750ml/1¹/₄pt water
2 cups/500ml/16fl oz lemon juice

Method:

1 *Place sugar and water in a saucepan over a low heat and cook, stirring, until sugar dissolves. Bring to the boil and boil for 30 seconds. Pour syrup into a heatproof bowl and chill.*

2 *Combine sugar syrup and lemon juice, pour into an ice-cream maker and freeze following manufacturer's instructions. Alternatively, pour mixture into a shallow freezerproof container and freeze until ice crystals start to form around the edges. Using a fork, stir to break up ice crystals. Repeat the process once more then freeze until firm.*

Serves 6

mango
sherbet

ingredients

2¹/₂ cups/625g/1¹/₄lb sugar
2 cups/500ml/16fl oz water
1¹/₂kg/3 lb fresh mango flesh

Method:

1 *Place sugar and water in a saucepan over a low heat and cook, stirring, until sugar dissolves. Bring to the boil and boil for 30 seconds. Pour syrup into a heatproof bowl and chill.*

2 *Place mango in a food processor and process until smooth. Push puréed mango through a fine sieve, then stir in syrup. Pour mango mixture into a ice-cream maker and freeze following manufacturer's instructions. Alternatively, pour mixture into a shallow freezerproof container and freeze until ice crystals start to form around the edges. Using a fork, stir to break up ice crystals. Repeat the process once more then freeze until firm.*

Serves 6

strawberry
ice

Method:

1 *Purée melon, strawberries, lemon juice, sugar and water in a blender or food processor.*

2 *Pour mixture into an ice cream maker and chill according to instructions. Alternatively, freeze in ice trays. When semi-frozen, beat the mixture to break up any large ice crystals. Repeat the process twice more, then freeze in a suitable container until solid.*

Serves 6

ingredients

**315g/10oz cantaloupe
melon flesh, chopped
185g/6oz strawberries, hulled
2 tablespoon lemon juice
60g/2oz sugar
125ml/4fl oz water**

---

tangy
lemon ice

Method:

1 *Combine water and sugar in a heavy saucepan and bring to the boil, stirring until sugar dissolves. Then simmer for 1-2 minutes or until a syrup forms. Remove from heat, stir in lemon juice and set aside to cool completely.*

2 *Pour mixture into a freezer container and freeze, beating occasionally with an electric mixer or whisk, until solid, or use an ice cream maker.*

**Makes approximately
4cups/1 litre/1³/₄ pints**

ingredients

**2 cups/500ml/16fl oz water
315g/10oz sugar
2 cups/500ml/16fl oz strained fresh
lemon juice**

pineapple
and mint sherbet

Photograph opposite

Method:

1 *Remove the skin and core from the pineapple. Finely chop ⅓ of the flesh and set aside.*
2 *Using a food processor or blender, purée remaining pineapple with the icing sugar and yoghurt.*
3 *Beat the egg whites until soft peaks form and fold into the pineapple together with chopped mint.*
4 *Pour into ice cream maker and churn approximately 30 minutes or until blades stop.*
  Note: *For a party, serve large scooped out pineapple shell with diced fresh pineapple and chopped mint. Chill. Just before serving top with pineapple sherbet and decorate.*

**Makes approximately
4 cups/1 litre/1³/₄ pints**

ingredients

**1 small pineapple or 750g/1¹/₂ lb can
pineapple pieces, drained
60g/2oz icing sugar
300ml/10oz plain unsweetened yoghurt
1 tablespoon chopped fresh mint
2 egg whites**

orange
sherbet

Method:

1 *Place zest in a fine strainer and pour boiling water over it. Drain, reserving zest.*
2 *In a saucepan over high heat, bring orange juice, sugar, 2 cups/500ml/16fl oz water, and lemon juice to a boil, stirring occasionally. Boil for 5 minutes. Remove from heat and let cool. Add orange zest.*
3 *Transfer to an ice cream machine and freeze according to manufacturer's instructions.*
  Note: *For an unusual and attractive presentation, pipe the sherbet through a pastry bag into chilled glass dishes or champagne glasses and refreeze until serving time. For a creamier texture, you can substitute skim milk for up to half of the juice.*

**Makes approximately
4 cups/1 litre/1³/₄ pints**

ingredients

**2 teaspoons orange zest
1 cup/250ml/8fl oz boiling water
4 cups/900ml/1¹/₂pt freshly squeezed
orange juice
2³/₄ cups/650g/22oz sugar
3 tablespoons lemon juice**

pear
sorbet

ingredients

**2 tablespoons lemon juice
1¹/₄ kg/2¹/₂lb fully ripe pears
4 cups/900ml/1¹/₂pts water
3 cups/750g/1¹/₂pts sugar
¹/₂ lemon, sliced
1 vanilla bean, split in half lengthwise
1-2 tablespoons lemon juice extra**

Method:

1 Stir the 2 tablespoons lemon juice into a bowl of cold water. Peel and core pears; place in lemon water.

2 Combine 3¹/₂ cups/800ml/1¹/₃pts water and 2¹/₂ cups/600ml/1pt of the sugar in a large saucepan. Stir over medium heat until sugar dissolves and syrup come to a boil. Reduce heat and add lemon, vanilla bean and pears. Cover and simmer 5 minutes. Turn pears over and simmer until tender (5-10 minutes, depending on ripeness of pears).

3 Drain pears, reserving poaching syrup. Let cool. Purée in food processor. Chill 1 cup /250ml/8fl oz of the poaching syrup, reserving any remaining syrup for another use.

4 Combine ¹/₃ cup/85ml/3fl oz water and the remaining sugar in a saucepan; stir over medium heat until syrup comes to the boil. Cool to room temperature; refrigerate until cold.

5 Combine the 1 cup/250ml/8fl oz reserved poaching syrup, the 1 tablespoon lemon juice, and pear purée. Then add half the cold sugar syrup. Taste and add more syrup if mixture is not sweet enough or more lemon juice if needed.

6 Freeze in ice cream machine according to manufacturer's instructions. Cover and store in freezer for up to 2 weeks.

**Makes approximately
4 cups/900ml/8fl oz**

celery
and tomato sorbet

Method:

1 *Using a food processor or blender, purée half of the tomato and celery. Place into a bowl. Purée remaining half together with the dill. Add to bowl.*

2 *Add vinegar, salt and pepper and stir to combine.*

3 *Whisk egg white until thick. Fold into tomato mixture.*

4 *Pour into ice cream maker and churn approximately 30 minutes or until blades stop.* **Note:** *Looks very attractive when served in hollowed out tomatoes.*

Makes approximately 4 cups/1 litre/1 ³/4 pints

ingredients

6 large tomatoes, peeled and quartered
4 stalks celery, strings removed and roughly chopped
1 tablespoon fresh chopped dill
1 tablespoon wine vinegar
1 tablespoon salt
¹/4 teaspoon pepper
1 egg white
parsley sprigs for garnish

nectarine
sorbet

Photograph opposite

ingredients

**4 cups/900g/1 1/2pts nectarines,
sliced and peeled
1/2 cup/125ml/4fl oz freshly squeezed
orange juice
sugar to taste
pinch salt
mint leaves, for garnish as needed**

nectarine sorbet

Method:

1 *Spread sliced nectarines in one layer on a baking sheet. Freeze, uncovered, until frozen solid.*

2 *Place frozen nectarines and orange juice in a blender or food processor. Process until smooth, stopping to scrape work bowl as necessary. If your machine struggles to process the frozen nectarines, let fruit stand 10-15 minutes at room temperature to thaw slightly. Depending on the size of your blender or food processor, you may have to process nectarines in several batches.*

3 *Add sugar to taste and salt. Mix thoroughly by hand or in food processor. Serve at once, garnished with mint leaves, or return to freezer for up to 1 hour.*

Note: *For a cool refreshing end to any meal, serve this tangy dessert garnished with fresh mint leaves.*

**Makes approximately
3 cups/750ml/24fl oz**

chocolate ice cream

ice creams

I scream, you scream, we all scream

for ice cream. As children we delighted in ice cream cones and sandwiches, sundaes and banana splits. As adults we still do. Ice Cream is a universal treat; travel just about anywhere and you can enjoy it with the natives. Birthday parties and afternoons at the beach absolutely demand it. Dinner party guests adore it. Whether it's shaped into an elaborate bombe, set aflame with brandy, topped with sauce, or just scooped into a cone, ice cream is a tasty, refreshing, happy dessert. With so many inexpensive, simple to operate and mess free ice cream machines now on the market, any home kitchen can be a first-class ice cream parlour, every dessert loving cook an ice cream pro.

fresh
peach ice cream

Photograph opposite

ingredients

3 fresh peaches, white or yellow
2 cups/500ml/16fl oz smoothy (see page
72 for recipe)
¹/₂ cup/120g/4oz sugar
¹/₂ teaspoon lemon juice
almond flavouring

Method:

1 *Peel the peaches after dipping into boiling water. Cut into small pieces. Add the sugar and leave to mature at room temperature for*

2 *Mix 1 cup of peaches and 1 cup of smoothy and blend until smooth. Fold into the remaining peach pieces and smoothy with the lemon juice and almond flavouring and chill.*

3 *Either churn or set by the freeze/beat method. Cover and ripen for one to two hours in the freezer, or until firm.*

Note: *Blending half the peaches helps to spread the flavour and adds colour, while the other half being left in pieces adds to the texture. Lemon juice is usually used with peaches to prevent them from browning. In this case, it is added later so that some discolouration takes place, because it is attractive in the ice cream.*

Makes approximately
4 cups/900ml/8fl oz

vanilla
ice cream

ingredients

4 cups/1 litre/35fl oz smoothy (see page 72
for recipe)
1¹/₄ cups/300g/10oz sugar
vanilla flavouring

Method:

1 *Mix all ingredients together and chill for one to two hours in the refrigerator.*

2 *Churn or set by the freeze/beat method and ripen, covered, in the freezer for two hours or until firm, before serving.*

Serves 8

rich
vanilla
ice cream

Method:

1 Beat the yolks and sugar until pale and frothy.

2 Heat smoothy in a medium-sized saucepan and stir constantly until custard thickens and coats the back of a wooden spoon. Add vanilla and leave to cool. Place a circle of greaseproof paper directly on top of the custard.

3 Whip the cream until it forms soft peaks, and fold into the thoroughly cooled custard. Pour into a wetted 3 cup/750ml/24fl oz mould and leave to set.

Note: Because this ice cream is so rich, it is not necessary to beat halfway through the setting period. This custard-based ice cream is a neutral base which can be used in a number of ways and flavoured in many different ways as well. If wanting to unmould this ice cream, first rinse the mould out with cold water, before pouring in the ice cream and freezing it.

To Unmould: Dip the mould into tepid water, invert over a serving dish and shake until the ice cream slips out. Return to the freezer to firm before garnishing and presenting.

**Makes approximately
3 cups/750mL/24fl oz**

ingredients

**4 egg yolks
²/₃ cup/160g/5oz sugar
I cup/250ml/8fl oz smoothy
(see page 72 for recipe)
I¹/₄cup/300ml/10fl oz thickened cream
vanilla flavouring**

white chocolate
and raspberry ice cream

Method:
1 *Place sugar and water in a small saucepan and cook over a low heat, stirring constantly until sugar dissolves. Bring to the boil, then reduce heat and simmer for 5 minutes or until syrup reduces by half.*
2 *Place egg yolks in a large mixing bowl and beat until thick and creamy. Continue beating, adding syrup in a thin stream. Add vanilla essence and chocolate and beat until mixture thickens and is cool.*
3 *Fold cream and raspberries into chocolate mixture. Place in a large freezerproof container, cover and freeze until firm.*

**Makes approximately
7cups/1750ml/3pts**

ingredients

**1¼ cups/315g/10oz sugar
½ cup/125ml/4fl oz water
6 egg yolks
1 teaspoon vanilla essence
250g/8oz white chocolate, melted
2 cups/500ml/16fl oz cream
(double), whipped
500g/1lb raspberries, roughly chopped**

chocolate
ice cream

Photograph opposite

ingredients

1 cup/220g/7oz caster sugar
9 egg yolks
1/2 cup/45g/1 1/2oz cocoa powder, sifted
2 cups/500ml/16fl oz milk
2 1/2 cups/600ml/1pt thickened cream
125g/4oz milk chocolate, melted

chocolate ice cream

Method:

1 *Place sugar and egg yolks in a bowl and beat until thick and pale.*
2 *Place cocoa powder in a saucepan. Gradually stir in milk and cream and heat over a medium heat, stirring constantly, until mixture is almost boiling. Stir in chocolate.*
3 *Remove pan from heat and whisk hot milk mixture into egg mixture. Set aside to cool.*
4 *Pour mixture into a freezerproof container and freeze for 30 minutes, or until mixture begins to freeze around edges. Beat mixture until even in texture. Return to freezer and repeat beating process two more times. Freeze until solid. Alternatively, place mixture in an ice cream maker and freeze according to manufacturer's instructions.*
Note: *For true chocoholics, chopped chocolate or chocolate bits can be folded into the mixture before it freezes solid. Serve in scoops with vanilla tuiles or raspberries.*

**Makes approximately
7cups/1750ml/3pts**

35

hazelnut
ice cream

Method:

1 Bring milk to the boil in a saucepan. Stir in hazelnuts, cream and vanilla; lower the heat so the mixture is just simmer.

2 Beat egg yolks with sugar until pale and creamy. Gradually add two thirds of the milk mixture, beating constantly.

3 Pour the contents of the mixing bowl into the remaining milk mixture in the pan. Cook over moderate heat, stirring constantly, until the mixture thickens enough to coat the back of a spoon. Cool.

4 Pour mixture into an ice cream maker and freeze according to instructions. Alternatively, freeze in ice trays. When semi-frozen, beat the mixture to break up any large ice crystals. Repeat the process twice more, then freeze in a suitable container until solid.

Serves 6

ingredients

500ml/16fl oz milk
110g/3¹/₂oz hazelnuts, ground
250ml/8fl oz double cream
2 teaspoon vanilla essence
6 egg yolks
185g/6oz soft brown sugar

mocha
ice cream

Method:

1 Combine the first 5 ingredients in the top of a double saucepan.

2 Stir over simmering water until chocolate has melted, cool.

3 Fold in evaporated milk and cream. Pour into ice cream machine. Churn until firm and blades stop turning. Approximately 40 minutes. Serve immediately or spoon into a container and freeze.

Note: If larger quantity required, double the ingredients listed above.

**Makes approximately
3 cups/³/₄ litre/1 ¹/₄pts**

ingredients

4 egg yolks
¹/₂ cup/120ml/4oz caster sugar
2 tablespoons coffee liqueur
1 tablespoon instant coffee powder
100g/3¹/₂oz dark chocolate, chopped
375ml/12¹/₂oz canned evaporated milk, chilled
1 cup/250ml/8fl oz cream, whipped

rich
chocolate ice cream

Method:

1 *Combine the first 4 ingredients in the top of a double saucepan.*
2 *Whisk over simmering water until chocolate has melted. Cool.*
3 *Whip evaporated milk until thick and fold into mixture with cream.*
4 *Pour into ice cream machine. Churn until firm and blades stop turning. (Approximately 40 minutes) Serve immediately or spoon into a container and freeze.*

**Makes approximately
3 cups/750ml/1 1/4pts**

ingredients

**4 egg yolks, lightly beaten
1/2 cup/120g/4oz castor sugar
2 tablespoons chocolate liqueur
200g/7oz dark chocolate, chopped
375ml/12 1/2oz can evaporated milk, chilled
1 cup/250ml/8fl oz cream, whipped**

mango
ice cream

Photograph opposite

ingredients

2 x 440g/14oz cans sliced mangoes, drained
4 tablespoon lemon juice
185g/6oz caster sugar
2 eggs, separated
300ml/10fl oz double cream, whipped

Method:

1 *Set aside a few mango slices for decoration. Purée mango with lemon juice and caster sugar in a blender or food processor. Transfer to a bowl. Cover. Refrigerate.*

2 *Using an electric mixer, beat egg yolks until pale and creamy. In a separate bowl, beat egg whites until stiff*

3 *Fold egg yolks into cream, then fold in mango purée. Finally, fold in stiffly beaten egg whites.*

4 *Spoon mixture into an ice cream maker and chill according to instructions. Alternatively, freeze in ice trays. When semi-frozen, beat the mixture to break up any large ice crystals. Repeat the process once more, then freeze in a suitable container until solid.*

5 *Soften slightly before serving, decorated with strawberries and the reserved mango slices.*

Makes approximately 4cups/1 litre/1³/₄ pts

pistachio
ice cream

ingredients

2 teaspoons gelatine
2 tablespoons boiling water
375ml/12¹/₂fl oz can evaporated milk, chilled
60g/2oz sugar
2 tablespoons Galliano
250g/8oz pistachio nuts, shelled, husked and chopped

Method:

1 *Dissolve gelatine in water. Whip evaporated milk, sugar, dissolved gelatine and Galliano until thick and frothy.*

2 *Stir in pistachio nuts. Pour into ice cream machine. Churn until firm and blades stop turning. (Approximately 40 minutes) Spoon into a container and freeze.*

Makes approximately 4cups/1 litre/1³/₄ pints

crunchy
caramel apricot sundae

ingredients

4 large scoops vanilla ice cream
440g/14oz canned apricots, drained

Crunchy caramel topping
30g/1oz unsalted butter
2 tablespoons brown sugar
60g/2oz toasted muesli
2 tablespoons walnuts, chopped
1 tablespoon shredded coconut

Method:

1 To make topping, place butter and sugar in a saucepan and cook, stirring, over a medium heat for 2-3 minutes or until sugar dissolves and mixture bubbles. Stir in muesli, nuts and coconut, mix well and remove pan from heat.

2 Place a scoop of ice cream in each serving dish, top with a few apricots and sprinkle with topping. Serve immediately.

Note: Any canned fruit can be used to make this easy dessert. The cooled topping will keep in an airtight container for several days.

Serves 4

rocky
road ice cream

Method:

1 Place ice cream in a large mixing bowl. Fold in Turkish Delight, pink and white marshmallows, red and green cherries, coconut and peanut bars. Spoon mixture into a freezerproof container, cover and freeze until firm.

Note: Serving suggestion: Place scoops of ice cream into bowls and serve with wafers.

**Makes approximately
6 cups/1 ¹/₂ litre/2 ¹/₂ pts**

ingredients

**1 litre/1 ³/₄ pt vanilla
ice cream, softened
2 x 60g/2oz chocolate-coated Turkish
Delight bars, chopped
10 pink marshmallows, chopped
5 white marshmallows, chopped
6 red glacé cherries, chopped
6 green glacé cherries, chopped
4 tablespoons shredded
coconut, toasted
2 x 45g/1 ¹/₂ oz chocolate-coated
scorched peanut bars, chopped**

strawberry
and cream ice cream

Photograph opposite

Method:
1 *Beat egg yolks and sugar until thick. Heat evaporated milk gently and then combine with egg yolk mixture.*
2 *Whisk over simmering water until slightly thickened. Cool.*
3 *Fold in remaining ingredients and pour into ice cream machine. Churn until firm and blades stop turning*
Makes approximately 4 cups/1 litre/1³/₄ pts

ingredients

3 egg yolks
¹/₄ cup/60g/2oz castor sugar
375ml/12¹/₂fl oz can evaporated milk
1 teaspoon vanilla essence
1 cup/250ml/8fl oz cream, whipped
1 punnet strawberries, hulled and quartered
4 tablespoons strawberry topping

boysenberry
swirl ice cream

Method:
1 *Beat egg yolks and sugar together.*
2 *Gently heat evaporated milk and combine with egg yolk mixture in the top of a double saucepan.*
3 *Whisk over simmering water until slightly thickened. Cool.*
4 *Add vanilla, half the boysenberries and cream.*
5 *Pour into ice cream machine. Churn until firm and blades stop turning.*
6 *Using a food processor or blender, purée remaining boysenberries with the dissolved gelatine. Spoon ice cream into a container and lightly fold in puréed boysenberries to give swirled appearance. Serve immediately or place in freezer.*
Makes approximately 4 cups/1 litre/1³/₄ pts

ingredients

4 egg yolks
¹/₂ cup caster sugar
375ml/13oz can evaporated milk
1 teaspoon vanilla essence
425g/14oz can boysenberries, drained
1 cup/250ml/8oz cream
1 teaspoon gelatine, dissolved in 1 tablespoon boiling water

frozen
nutty choc terrine

1 In a large heatproof bowl, melt milk chocolate with the chocolate and hazelnut spread. Cool slightly, stir in Tia Maria and egg yolks. Whip half the cream until soft peaks form. Fold into chocolate mixture.

2 Beat egg whites in a bowl until soft peaks form. Gradually add sugar, beating until mixture is stiff.

3 Melt dark chocolate; fold half into creamy chocolate mixture, then fold in the egg whites. Keep remaining chocolate warm over hot water.

4 Spoon mixture into a large loaf tin lined with cling film. Freeze until firm.

5 Make sauce by adding the remaining cream to the reserved chocolate. Stir over low heat until smooth. Serve with the sliced terrine.

Serves 12

ingredients

300g/9¹/₂oz milk chocolate
250g/8oz chocolate and hazelnut spread
60ml/2fl oz Tia Maria
6 eggs, separated
600ml/1pt double cream
3 tblspn caster sugar
250g/8oz dark chocolate

cinnamon
ice cream

Method:

1 Combine milk, cream, cinnamon stick and ground cinnamon in a heavy saucepan and heat over a very low heat, without boiling, for 15 minutes. Cover and cool to room temperature. Discard cinnamon stick.

2 Dissolve sugar in water over low heat, bring to the boil and boil rapidly until syrup reaches 120°C/250°F when tested with a sugar thermometer, or until a little syrup dropped into cold water will form a hard ball.

3 Beat egg yolks until thick and creamy then gradually add boiling syrup in a thin, steady stream, beating constantly until mixture is cold, thick and fluffy. Add cinnamon liquid and mix well.

4 Pour mixture into a freezer container and freeze, stirring or whisking mixture several times, until solid, or use an ice cream maker.
Note: Serve with hot peaches either poached or gently fried in a little butter with sugar.

Makes approximately 4 cups/1 litre/1 ³/₄ pts

ingredients

315ml/10fl oz milk
200ml/6 ¹/₂ fl oz double cream
1 stick cinnamon
1 tablespoon freshly ground cinnamon
125g/4oz sugar
200ml/6 ¹/₂ fl oz water
6 egg yolks

coconut
ice cream

Method:

1 Combine cream, milk and coconut in a saucepan and heat over a very low heat, without boiling, for 15 minutes. Cover and cool to room temperature. Blend mixture briefly in a food processor then strain through a sieve, rubbing to extract as much liquid as possible from the coconut. Discard coconut pulp.

2 Beat eggs, egg yolks, sugar and salt in a heatproof bowl until thick. Place over simmering water, add coconut liquid and cook, stirring, until slightly thickened. Remove from heat, place over a pan of iced water and allow to cool, stirring occasionally.

3 Pour mixture into a freezer container, cover and freeze until firm. Scoop into bowls and decorate with lightly toasted shredded coconut.

Makes approximately 4 cups/1 litre /1 ³/₄ pt

ingredients

375ml/12fl oz double cream
375ml/12fl oz milk
90g/3oz desiccated coconut
2 eggs
2 egg yolks
125g/4oz sugar
pinch salt
toasted shredded coconut for serving

creamy
honey ice cream

Photograph opposite

ingredients

3 egg yolks
1 egg
375ml/13oz can evaporated milk
200ml/7oz honey
300ml/10fl oz cream, whipped

Method:

1 *Combine egg yolks and egg in the top of a double saucepan. Beat until light and fluffy.*
2 *Heat evaporated milk in a separate saucepan until lukewarm.*
3 *Stir in honey and gradually whisk into egg mixture. Stir constantly over simmering heat.*
4 *Remove from heat and cool. Fold through whipped cream.*
5 *Pour into ice cream machine. Churn until firm and blades stop turning. Approximately 40 minutes. Serve immediately or spoon into a container and freeze.*

Makes approximately 4 cups/1 litre/1 3/4 pts

caramel
ice cream

ingredients

375ml/13oz can evaporated milk
1/2 cup/120ml/4oz caramel sauce
1/2 cup/90g/3oz crushed toffee

Method:

1 *Whip evaporated milk and caramel sauce together until thick and frothy.*
2 *Fold in crushed toffee.*
3 *Pour into ice cream machine. Churn until firm and blades stop turning (approximately 30 minutes). Spoon into a container and freeze.*
Note: *If larger quantity required, double the ingredients listed above.*

Makes approximately 2 cups/1/2 litre/16fl oz

pernod
and peach ice cream

Method:

1 Put peaches in a bowl and cover with boiling water. Drain after 15 seconds and remove the skins.
2 Cut the peaches into quarters, discarding the stones.
3 Put the sugar and water into a heavy based saucepan and heat gently until sugar dissolves. Increase the heat and cook rapidly for 5 minutes.
4 Purée the peaches together with the syrup and stir in the Pernod and yoghurt.
5 Beat the cream until soft peaks form and fold into fruit mixture.
6 Pour into ice cream maker and churn approximately 30 minutes or until blades stop.

Makes 4 cups/1 litre/1 3/4 pts

ingredients

4-5 fresh peaches
1/2 cup/125g/4oz caster sugar
300ml/10fl oz water
2 tablespoons Pernod
300ml/10fl oz plain unsweetened yoghurt
150ml/5fl oz thickened cream

morello
cherry ice cream

Method:

1 *Chop the cherries (medium fine) and stir all ingredients together, making sure the sugar is dissolved. Chill.*

2 *Either churn or set by the freeze/beat method. Cover and ripen in the freezer until firm.*

**Makes approximately
3 ¹/₂ cups/900ml/1 ¹/₂pts**

ingredients

2 cups/500ml/16fl oz smoothy (see page 72
for recipe)

²/₃ cup/150g/5oz pitted Morello cherries,
drained

¹/₂ cup/120ml/4fl oz syrup from cherries

2 tablespoons cherry brandy, optional

¹/₃ cup/80g/3oz sugar

few drops red food colouring

fresh
fig ice cream

Photograph opposite

ingredients

200g/7oz fresh ripe figs, white or purple
1/2 cup/120g/4oz sugar
2 cups/500ml/16fl oz smoothy (see page 72 for recipe)

Method:
1 *Peel and chop figs roughly, cook slowly with sugar for 10 minutes, stirring from time to time to dissolve sugar and prevent catching.*
2 *Purée in blender of food processor and cool.*
3 *Add to smoothy and mix well. Chill.*
4 *Either churn or set by the freeze/beat method. Cover and ripen in freezer for one to two hours or until firm. Garnish with chocolate curls or grated chocolate.*
Makes approximately
3 1/2 cups/900ml/1 1/2pts

apple-pie
ice cream

ingredients

2 cups/500ml/16fl oz smoothy (see page 72 for recipe)
3/4 cup/180g/6oz bottled apple sauce
sugar, optional
150ml/5fl oz thickened cream
pinch ground cloves
1/8 teaspoon cinnamon
1/2 teaspoon green food colouring

Method:
1 *Mix all ingredients together and chill.*
2 *Either churn or set by the freeze/beat method. Cover and ripen in the freezer for one hour, or until firm.*
3 *Before serving, rest in the bottom of the refrigerator if too firm.*
Makes approximately
3 1/2 cups/850ml/1 1/3pts

chocolate
brandy ice cream

Photograph opposite

1 Combine the cream, milk, chocolate and coffee in a large saucepan over moderate heat. Stir until the chocolate melts, do not allow mixture to boil.
2 Meanwhile, using an electric mixer, beat egg yolks with sugar until pale and thick. Continue to beat while adding hot mocha cream. Return mixture to a clean pan and stir constantly over moderate heat until mixture thickens slightly. Stir in brandy. Set aside until cool.
3 Pour mixture into an ice cream maker and chill according to instructions. Alternatively, freeze in ice trays. When semi-frozen, beat mixture to break up any large ice crystals. Repeat the process twice more, then freeze in a suitable container until solid.

Serves 12

ingredients

750ml/1¼pt double cream
250ml/8fl oz milk
155g/5oz dark chocolate, grated
2 teaspoon instant coffee powder
5 egg yolks
185g/6oz caster sugar
2 tablespoon brandy

quick
chocolate chip ice cream

Method:
1 Whip cream with Kahlua until soft peaks form; fold mixture into ice cream. Spoon into a freezerproof container and freeze until semi-frozen.
2 Beat mixture to break up any large ice crystals. Stir in chocolate chips and nuts. Freeze until solid.

Serves 12

ingredients

Chop the nuts very finely.
A food processor,
250ml/8fl oz double cream
3 tblspn Kahlua
2 litres/3½pt good quality vanilla ice cream, softened
250g/8oz chocolate chips
125g/4oz almonds, chopped

chocolate pear bombe

special treats

Frozen desserts always seem special.

For adults, ice cream desserts, especially those laced with luscious liqueurs, are the perfect endings for stylish dinnerparties or romantic evenings. Frozen drinks are refreshing on lazy summer afternoons, bringing with them memories - or dreams - of vacations in exotic, tropical places. For children, frozen treats mean birthday parties, days at the beach and the ice cream truck coming down the street at last. Ice cream has a way of adding sparkle to any occasion. What could be more fun to eat than birthday cake and ice cream?

watermelon
bombe

Photograph opposite

ingredients

**French vanilla ice milk base
(see page 72)
1/4 cup/60ml miniature semisweet
chocolate chips
900ml/1 quart purchased raspberry
sherbet, slightly softened
green food colouring, as needed**

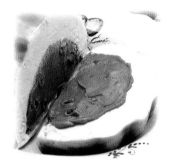

watermelon bombe

Method:

1 *Chill a 1 4/5 litre/2 quart melon-shaped mold in the freezer for at least 1 hour.*

2 *Line inside of mold with a layer of Vanilla Ice Milk. Cover with plastic film, pressing against the ice milk to seal it tightly and fill any air pockets. Return mold to freezer for at least 4 hours.*

3 *Stir chocolate chips into raspberry sherbet to simulate watermelon seeds. Remove plastic wrap from mold and fill cavity with sherbet. Top with plastic film and freeze until firm.*

4 *To unmold, dip mold quickly in lukewarm water and invert onto a chilled platter. Return to freezer to set.*

5 *Paint outside of molded ice milk with green food colouring. Cover well and return to freezer. Slice to serve.*

Note: *This molded dessert looks like a miniature watermelon. It's a treat for the eyes as well as the palate. The bombe must freeze in stages, so preparation must begin early on the day it will be served, or even the day before.*

Serves 10

coffee
granita

ingredients

**500ml/16fl oz hot strong black coffee
sugar to taste
freshly whipped double cream,
sweetened to taste**

Method:

1 *While the coffee is still piping hot, stir in sugar until dissolved. Cool completely, then chill thoroughly.*
2 *Pour mixture into a freezer container and freeze, beating with an electric mixer or processing mixture several times, until solid, or use an ice cream maker.*
3 *For easier serving, break up granita, place in a food processor and process to a fine textured soft ice. Spoon into chilled goblets and garnish with cream.*

**Makes approximately
2 1/2 cups/600ml/1 pint**

macadamia
nut ice cream

ingredients

**2 cups/500ml/16fl oz smoothy
(see page 72 for recipe)
1 1/2 cups/180g/6oz shelled macadamia nuts
1/3 cup/80g/3oz sugar
few grains salt
almond flavouring, optional**

Method:

1 *Chop the nuts very finely. A food processor, blender or nut mill are the most efficient. Otherwise, using a large board, a large knife and lots of patience, chop the nuts and add to the smoothy in a medium-sized saucepan and bring very slowly to the boil. Turn off the heat, put on lid and infuse for five minutes.*
2 *Stir in sugar and salt, optional flavouring and cool. Chill.*
3 *Either churn or set by the freeze/beat method. Cover and ripen in the freezer for one to two hours before serving.*

Serves 5-6

ice cream
christmas pudding

Method:

1 Place ice cream, apricots, cherries, pears, sultanas, raisins and rum in a bowl and mix to combine. Pour into an oiled and lined 6 cup/1 1/2 litre/2 1/2pt capacity pudding basin.

2 Freeze for 3 hours or until firm.

Note: To help unmould the pudding, briefly hold a warm, damp teatowel around the outside of the mould. Slice pudding and serve with rum custard.

Serves 8

ingredients

1 litre/1 3/4 pt chocolate ice cream, softened
125g/4oz glacé apricots, chopped
125g/4oz glacé cherries, chopped
125g/4oz glacé pears, chopped
90g/3oz sultanas
75g/2 1/2oz raisins, chopped
2 tablespoons rum

chocolate-
pear bombe

Photograph opposite

ingredients

Pear Ice Milk
¹/₃ cup/85ml/3oz sugar
2 tablespoons lemon juice
I tablespoon pear-flavoured liqueur
I tablespoon grated lemon zest
850ml/29oz can pear halves,
packed in natural juice or water,
drained, puréed and chilled

500ml/I pint Chocolate Ice Milk
I ¹/₂ litre/I ¹/₂ quarts Vanilla Ice Milk
whipped light cream and chocolate
shavings, for garnish (optional)
as needed

chocolate-pear bombe

Method:

1 *In a saucepan heat sugar with ¹/₃ cup /85ml water until sugar melts. Remove from heat and cool. Add lemon juice, liqueur, and lemon zest. Chill. Stir sugar syrup into chilled pear purée. Transfer to an ice cream machine and freeze according to manufacturer's instructions. Let ice milk "ripen" in freezer for several hours.*

2 *Chill a I ¹/₂ litre/I ¹/₂ quart mold in the freezer for several hours or overnight. Press three quarters of the chocolate ice milk into the mold, evenly covering the sides and bottom. Cover with plastic film, pressing against the ice milk to seal it tightly and fill any air pockets. Freeze until firm.*

3 *Press the Vanilla Ice Milk into an even layer over the Chocolate Ice Milk. Cover and freeze until very firm.*

4 *Fill in the centre of the bombe with the Pear Ice Milk. Freeze until very firm.*

5 *Cover the top surface with the remaining Chocolate Ice Milk. Cover with plastic film and freeze overnight or until ice milk is very firm.*

6 *To unmold, dip mold quickly in lukewarm water and invert onto a chilled serving plate. Return to freezer to set. Before serving, decorate the bombe with whipped cream and chocolate shavings, if used.*

Note: *This elegant bombe boasts two luscious ice-milk layers surrounding a creamy pear sorbet centre.*

Serves IO

tia maria
and chocolate ice cream

Method:

1 *Heat fresh cream and vanilla. Add ½ grated chocolate to mixture and melt.*

2 *Whisk egg yolks and sugar together - pour on chocolate cream and beat - reheat until thickened. Cool.*

3 *Add remainder of chocolate, Tia Maria, thickened cream and grated orange rind. Pour into ice cream maker and churn, approximately 30 minutes or until blades stop.*

**Makes approximately
4cups/1 litre /1¾pt**

ingredients

**45ml/1½oz standard fresh cream
3 drops vanilla essence
3 egg yolks
100g/3⅓oz castor sugar
1 cup/120g/4oz grated cooking
chocolate
2 tablespoons Tia Maria
150ml/5fl oz thickened cream
1 teaspoon grated orange rind**

grand
marnier and cream

Method:

1 In a heavy-based saucepan combine sugar, orange juice, water and peel. Stir constantly over a medium heat until mixture comes to a boil. Cook rapidly for 5 minutes. Set aside.

2 Beat egg yolks until fluffy and pale lemon coloured. Beating constantly, pour hot syrup over beaten egg yolks. Continue beating and cook over hot water until mixture is very thick; then cool.

3 Fold in Grand Marnier liqueur.

4 Whip cream until soft peaks form and fold into egg mixture. Pour into ice cream maker and churn approximately 30 minutes or until blades stop.

Makes 4cups/l litre/l ³/₄ pts

ingredients

¹/₂ **cup/125g/4oz sugar**
¹/₄ **cup/60ml/2 fl oz orange juice**
¹/₂ **cup/125ml/4oz water**
1 teaspoon grated orange peel
8 egg yolks
¹/₄ **cup/60ml/2 fl oz Grand Marnier liqueur**
1 cup/250ml/8oz whipping cream

party friend
ice creams

Method:

1 Cut through the cones where the cup joins the cornet "handle" and place the cup upside down on a baking tray covered with foil.

2 Place a scoop of firm ice cream on the inverted cup. Scatter over chocolate nonpareilles or coconut to make hair. Using a small rose piping tube, pipe cream around the base of the ice cream or leave plain.

3 To make the hats, dip the base of the cornet into glace icing or melted chocolate, turning to coat approximately 2¹/₂cm/1in, up the cone. Then dip into chocolate nonpareilles, or leave plain.

4 When the cornet is dry, decorate by sticking a row of three Smarties down one side using melted chocolate or very stiff glace icing.
Place cornet on ice cream at a jaunty angle and form faces with jubes, etc.

5 Place tray in the freezer until ready to serve.

Make 1 party friend per child

ingredients

**scoops of vanilla, chocolate and
strawberry ice cream
cornet ice cream cones
Smarties
chocolate nonpareilles
multi-coloured nonpareilles
desiccated coconut
life savers
coloured jubes
cooking chocolate, melted
glace icing (icing sugar mixed with
thickened cream)
thickened cream, whipped**

chocolate
hazelnut meringue baskets

Method:

1 Preheat oven to 150°C/300°F/Gas 2. Cut 2 pieces of nonstick baking parchment to fit two baking sheets. Invert the baking parchment and draw four circles on each piece, each measuring 7½cm/3in in diameter. Replace the parchment, pencilled side down.

2 In a large heatproof bowl, whisk egg whites with salt until stiff. Whisk in icing sugar, 1 tablespoon at a time. Place the bowl over a saucepan of gently simmering water; continue to whisk for about 5 minutes until meringue is stiff.

3 Spoon meringue into a piping bag fitted with a fluted nozzle and, starting in the centre of each circle, pipe 6 individual meringue baskets, using a spiral action and making the sides three spirals high.

4 Bake meringue baskets for 1¼-1½ hours. Cool on a wire rack, then store in an airtight tin.

5 Make ice cream. Combine sugar, milk and cream in a saucepan. Bring to the boil, stirring to dissolve the sugar. Remove from the heat. In a bowl, beat egg yolks lightly. Add scalded cream mixture in a thin stream, beating constantly to make a light foamy mixture. Transfer to the top of a double boiler (or a heatproof bowl) and place over simmering water. Stir until custard coats the back of a spoon, then pour into a clean bowl and chill in a larger bowl filled with ice. As soon as custard is cool, cover it closely and refrigerate for 2 hours.

6 Fold in ground hazelnuts. Pour into an ice cream maker and chill according to instructions, adding the chopped nuts and chocolate chips when churning is almost complete. Alternatively, freeze in ice trays. When semi-frozen, beat mixture to break up any large ice crystals. Repeat theprocess twice more, adding the chopped hazelnuts and chocolate chips during the final beating. Freeze in a suitable container until ice cream is solid.

7 About 30 minutes before serving, transfer the ice cream to the refrigerator to soften slightly. Make the chocolate sauce. Melt chocolate with butter in a heavy-based saucepan. Gradually beat in cream and warm through, stirring constantly.

8 Arrange the meringue baskets on individual plates. Place 2 scoops of ice cream in each basket, then top each scoop of ice cream with hot chocolate sauce. Serve at once.

Kitchen tips:

For a quick cheat's pudding use a good quality bought ice cream (coffee is delicious). Don't be tempted to use bought meringue baskets, however, unless you have access to a good baker. The super-sweet, dry meringues sold in packs in supermarkets are not suitable. Make a plain vanilla ice cream by omitting the hazelnuts and adding 2 teaspoons natural vanilla essence. Before scooping it into the meringue baskets, fill them with strawberrries or raspberries for a summer treat.

Serves 6

ingredients

4 egg whites
pinch salt
280g/9oz icing sugar

Ice cream
125g/4oz caster sugar
300ml/10fl oz milk
600ml/1pt double cream
8 egg yolks
155g/5oz ground hazelnuts
60g/2oz toasted hazelnuts, chopped
90g/3oz chocolate chips

Chocolate sauce
185g/6oz plain chocolate
60g/2oz butter
185ml/6fl oz double cream
vanilla essence (optional)

cassata
layers

ingredients

1 x 20cm/8in sponge cake
¼ cup/60ml/2fl oz almond-flavoured liqueur
chocolate curls

Cassata filling
1 litre/1¾pt vanilla ice cream, softened
1 cup/250ml/8fl oz cream (double)
125g/4oz glacé apricots, chopped
125g/4oz glacé pineapple, chopped
60g/2oz glacé cherries, chopped
60g/2oz raisins, halved
125g/4oz dark chocolate, grated
125g/4oz pistachio nuts, chopped

Method:

1 *To make filling place ice cream, cream, apricots, pineapple, cherries, raisins, chocolate and pistachio nuts in a bowl and mix to combine.*

2 *Split sponge horizontally into three even layers. Place one layer of sponge in the base of a lined 20cm/8in springform tin and sprinkle with 1 tablespoon of liqueur. Top with one-third of the filling. Repeat layers to use all ingredients ending with a layer of filling. Freeze for 5 hours or until firm. Remove from freezer 1 hour before serving and place in refrigerator.*

3 *Just prior to serving, decorate with chocolate curls.*

Note: Use the best quality ice cream you can afford. To retain maximum volume and creamy texture, keep the cassata filling mixture well chilled until the cassata is finally assembled.

Serves 10

nougat
tartufo

Method:

1 Place nougat, hazelnuts, almonds, chocolate, ice cream and honey in a bowl and mix carefully to combine.

2 Spoon ice cream mixture into eight 1 cup/250ml/ 8fl oz capacity chilled aluminium moulds lined with plastic food wrap and freeze for 1 hour.

3 Remove moulds from freezer and unmould. Roll ice cream in coconut. Place on a tray lined with plastic food wrap, cover and freeze until required.

Note: To toast nuts, place them in a single layer on a baking tray or in a shallow ovenproof dish and bake at 180°C/350°F/ Gas 4 for 10-15 minutes or until they are golden. Turn them several times during cooking. Set aside to cool.

Serves 8

ingredients

¹/₂ cup/125g/4oz sugar
200g/6¹/₂oz nougat, chopped
60g/2oz hazelnuts, toasted and chopped
6g/2oz slivered almonds, toasted
200g/6¹/₂oz dark or milk chocolate, chopped
2 litres/3¹/₂pt vanilla ice cream, softened
3 tablespoons honey
¹/₂ cup/45g/1¹/₂oz shredded coconut, toasted

cassata
log

Photograph opposite

cassata log

ingredients

¹/₂ cup/100g/3¹/₂oz caster sugar
2 tablespoons water
315g/10oz ricotta cheese, drained
90g/3oz dark chocolate, chopped
45g/1¹/₂oz mixed glacé cherries
2 tablespoons chopped candied
mixed peel
2 tablespoons crushed nuts
2 tablespoons sweet sherry
1¹/₂ cups/375mL/12fl oz cream
(double), whipped

Method:

1 Place sugar and water in a saucepan and bring to the boil over a medium heat, stirring until sugar dissolves. Reduce heat and simmer, without stirring, for 2 minutes. Remove pan from heat and set aside to cool slightly.

2 Push ricotta cheese through a fine sieve into a large bowl. Slowly stir sugar syrup into cheese, mixing well to combine. Add chocolate, cherries, mixed peel, nuts and sherry and mix to combine. Fold in cream.

3 Spoon mixture into a foil-lined 11x21cm/ 4¹/₂x8¹/₂in loaf tin. Cover with foil and freeze overnight. To serve, unmould and cut into slices.

Note: Delicious served with thick cream and savoiardi biscuits (sponge fingers) or topped with purchased chocolate topping.

Serves 6

apricot
yoghurt ice cream

Method:

1 *Place the first 7 ingredients into a saucepan. Stir over heat until sugar dissolves. Bring to the boil. Simmer 20 minutes, or until apricots are tender. Cool.*

2 *Strain, reserving 1 cup of liquid. Discard cloves and cinnamon stick.*

3 *Using a food processor or blender, purée apricots and liquid together.*

4 *Stir in yoghurt and evaporated milk.*

5 *Pour into ice cream machine. Churn until firm and blades stop turning. (Approximately 40 minutes) Serve immediately or spoon into a container and freeze.*

**Makes approximately
4 cups/1 litre /1³/₄pt**

ingredients

**375g/13oz dried apricots
1 cinnamon stick
¹/₂ teaspoon grated nutmeg
3 cloves
1 cup/155g/5oz brown sugar
¹/₃ cup/100g/3oz honey
2 cups/500ml/16oz water
1 cup/250ml/8oz natural yoghurt
375ml/13oz evaporated milk, chilled**

yoghurt
passionfruit ice cream

Method:

1 Combine the honey and yoghurt in a bowl; mix well. Dissolve the gelatine in the water. Cool slightly, then stir into the yoghurt mixture. Freeze in ice trays until firm.

2 Transfer the frozen yoghurt mixture to a large bowl. Using a hand-held electric mixer, beat until the mixture doubles in bulk.

3 Beat the egg white in a grease-free bowl until stiff peaks form. Fold into the yoghurt mixture with the passionfruit pulp. Freeze in a freezerproof container until firm. Decorate with passionfruit pulp.

Serves 4

ingredients

2 tablespoons clear honey
215ml/7fl oz natural low fat yoghurt
1 teaspoon powdered gelatine
2 tablespoons water
1 egg white
pulp of 1 passionfruit, plus extra to decorate

yoghurt
orange ice cream

Method:

1 Combine the honey and yoghurt in a large bowl; mix well. Dissolve gelatine in the water. Cool slightly, then stir into yoghurt mixture.

2 Line a loaf tin with cling film. Spoon yoghurt mixture into the tin, cover and freeze for 3 hours.

3 Beat the frozen mixture in a large bowl until doubled in bulk. Beat in the vanilla, orange rind and juice.

4 Whisk the egg whites to soft peaks in a separate, grease-free bowl. Fold into the yoghurt ice, return the mixture to the loaf tin, cover and freeze until solid. Soften slightly before serving- with fresh fruit.

Serves 6-8

ingredients

4 tablespoons clear honey
375ml/12fl oz orange-flavoured yoghurt
1 tablespoon powdered gelatine
60ml/2fl oz water
1 teaspoon vanilla essence
2 teaspoon finely grated orange rind
2 tablespoons freshly squeezed orange juice
2 egg whites

french
vanilla ice milk base

Photograph opposite

Method:

1 *In a heavy-based saucepan, heat milk, sugar, and vanilla bean. (If you are using vanilla extract, do not add it until step 4). Stir occasionally until sugar is dissolved and the mixture is hot but not boiling.*

2 *Whisk egg yolks together in a bowl. Continue whisking and very slowly pour in approximately 1 cup/250ml/8oz of the milk mixture. When smooth, pour back into the pan.*

3 *Whisk constantly over low heat until the mixture thickens slightly and coats the back of a spoon (about 5 minutes). Take care that the mixture doesn't boil, or it will curdle. Draw your finger across the back of the coated spoon. If the line you make remains, the custard is done.*

4 *Remove vanilla bean; or, if you're using vanilla extract, add it at this stage.*

5 *Strain into a clean bowl and cool thoroughly.*

6 *Transfer to an ice cream machine and freeze according to manufacturer's instructions.*

ingredients

4¼ cups/960ml/32 fl oz skim milk
¾ cup/185g/6oz sugar
2 vanilla beans or
2 tablespoons vanilla extract
2 egg yolks

Note: *Increase vanilla in the above recipe to 2 vanilla beans or 2 tablespoons vanilla extract. This recipe is recommended as the foundation for some of the ice creams in this book. It produces consistently excellent flavour and texture. The same ingredients combined in different proportions give somewhat different results. Experiment to find which combination of ingredients is most appealing to your palate. Vanilla beans will give a richer flavour than extract.*

**Makes approximately
4 cups/900ml/32fl oz**

smoothy
base

Method:

1 *Dissolve the skim milk powder in the milk and then gently blend the cream into the mixture.*

2 *The mixture should be chilled and well stirred before use in ice cream making.*

ingredients

750ml/25oz milk
225ml/7fl oz thickened (double) cream
30g/1oz instant skim milk powder

simple
sugar syrup

ingredients

2 cups/500g/16oz sugar
1 cup/250ml/8oz water

Method:

1 *In a medium sized saucepan, cook sugar and the water over high heat, stirring constantly, until sugar dissolves and mixture reaches a full, rolling boil.*

2 *Immediately remove from heat and cool to room temperature. Strain through a fine sieve into a jar or bowl. Cover and refrigerate until needed. Sugar syrup should always be well cooled to about 4°C/40°F before being used.*

Makes about 3 cups

The Stages of Cooked Sugar Syrup

Simple syrup - The sugar has dissolved. The syrup is clear and registers about 104°C /215°F on a candy thermometer.

Soft-ball stage - 120°C/234°- 240°F. A small spoonful of syrup dropped into ice water then rubbed between finger and thumb forms a soft ball.

Caramel stage - 180°C/320° t o 3 5 5 ° F. The syrup turns golden brown.

Note: *This traditional syrup falls somewhere between French and Italian. It may be stored in the refrigerator for several weeks.*

simple syrup

soft-ball stage

caramel stage

make your own
ice cream cones

ingredients

1 cup/250g/8oz unsalted butter
6 eggs
1¹/₂ cups/375g/12oz sugar
2 tablespoons vanilla extract
3¹/₂ cups/440g/14oz flour
4 teaspoons baking powder

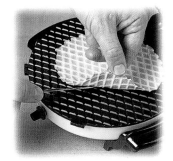

Method:

1 *Melt butter over low heat; let cool. Beat eggs with an electric mixer. While beating, add sugar in a steady stream; continue beating until smooth. Add cooled butter and vanilla extract, then mix in flour and baking powder.*

2 *Bake in pizzelle iron according to manufacturer's instructions.*

3 *Lift the edges of the hot pizzelle with a knife and carefully peel it from the iron.*

4 *Roll one side toward the centre to begin forming a cone.*

5 *Wrap the opposite side around to complete the cone shape. Pinch the overlapping edges together.*

Makes approximately 50

fresh
fruit sauces

Colourful and refreshing, low-fat dessert sauces are a welcome change from rich toppings and gooey syrups laden with butter or cream. Made with a variety of fresh seasonal or frozen fruits and a few other simple ingredients you probably already have on hand in your refrigerator or pantry, these sauces are ideal for impromptu entertaining or a quiet night at home. They take only minutes to make in a blender or food processor; they complement most any ice cream, sherbet, sorbet, or ice; and best of all, you can make them as sweet or tart, as thick or thin as you like.

Melon-Berry Sauce

2 chilled cantaloupes
1 cup/250g/8oz fresh strawberries
1 teaspoon freshly squeezed lemon or lime juice
1/8 teaspoon grated nutmeg or freshly grated ginger
light sour cream or yoghurt, for garnish (optional) as needed

1 *Halve and seed melons. Scoop out flesh, discarding shells. Using a blender or food processor and working in batches, purée melon and strawberries until smooth.*
2 *Add lemon juice and nutmeg and stir briefly to blend. Pour into serving dish and garnish with sour cream, if desired. Serve at once or refrigerate, covered, for up to 4 hours before serving.*
Makes 3 cups/700ml/23fl oz
4 servings

Just-a-Bowl-of-Cherries Sauce

3 cups/700ml pitted sweet red cherries
1/2 cup/125ml fresh or bottled pomegranate juice
honey or sugar (optional) to taste
1/2 teaspoon almond or vanilla extract
light sour cream or non-fat yoghurt, for garnish (optional) as needed

1 *Using a blender and working in batches, purée cherries with pomegranate juice until smooth.*
2 *Sweeten mixture with honey or sugar to taste, if desired; add almond extract and blend briefly to mix well. Pour into serving dish and garnish with sour cream, if desired. Serve at once or refrigerate, covered, for up to 4 hours before serving.*
Makes 3 cups/700mL/23fl oz
4 servings

Kiwi-Nectarine Sauce

2 1/2 cups/600ml peeled, chopped kiwifruit
1 nectarine or peach, pitted and quartered
currant or mint jelly to taste
light sour cream or non-fat yoghurt (optional) as needed

1 *Using a blender and working in batches, purée kiwifruit with nectarine or peach until smooth.*
2 *Stir in jelly to taste and blend briefly to mix well. Pour into serving dish and garnish with sour cream, if desired. Serve at once or refrigerate, covered, for up to 4 hours before serving.*
Makes 3 cups/700ml/23fl oz
4 servings

Cooking is not an exact science: one does not require finely calibrated scales, pipettes and scientific equipment to cook, yet the conversion to metric measures in some countries and its interpretations must have intimidated many a good cook.

Weights are given in the recipes only for ingredients such as meats, fish, poultry and some vegetables. Though a few grams/ounces one way or another will not affect the success of your dish.

Though recipes have been tested using the Australian Standard 250ml cup, 20ml tablespoon and 5ml teaspoon, they will work just as well with the US and Canadian 8fl oz cup, or the UK 300ml cup. We have used graduated cup measures in preference to tablespoon measures so that proportions are always the same. Where tablespoon measures have been given, these are not crucial measures, so using the smaller tablespoon of the US or UK will not affect the recipe's success. At least we all agree on the teaspoon size.

For breads, cakes, pastries, etc the only area which might cause concern is where eggs are used, as proportions will then vary. If working with a 250ml or 300ml cup, use large eggs (60g/2oz), adding a little more liquid to the recipe for 300ml cup measures if it seems necessary. Use the medium-sized eggs (55g/1 ^{1}/$_{4}$oz) with 8fl oz cup measure. A graduated set of measuring cups and spoons is recommended, the cups in particular for measuring dry ingredients. Remember to level such ingredients.

English measures

All measurements are similar to Australian with two exceptions: the English cup measures 300ml/10floz, whereas the Australian cup measure 250mL/8fl ozs. The English tablespoon (the Australian dessertspoon) measures 14.8ml against the Australian tablespoon of 20ml.

American measures

The American reputed pint is 16fl oz, a quart is equal to 32fl oz and the American gallon, 128fl oz. The Imperial measurement is 20fl oz to the pint, 40fl oz a quart and 160 fl oz one gallon.

The American tablespoon is equal to 14.8ml, the teaspoon is 5mL. The cup measure is 250ml/8fl oz, the same as Australia.

Dry measures

All the measures are level, so when you have filled a cup or spoon, level it off with the edge of a knife. The scale below is the "cook's equivalent", it is not an exact conversion of metric to imperial measurement.

The exact metric equivalent is 2.2046lb = 1kg or 1lb = 0.45359kg

Metric		Imperial	
g = grams		oz = ounces	
kg = kilograms		lb = pound	
15g		^{1}/$_{2}$oz	
20g		^{2}/$_{3}$oz	
30g		1oz	
60g		2oz	
90g		3oz	
125g		4oz	^{1}/$_{4}$lb
155g		5oz	
185g		6oz	
220g		7oz	
250g		8oz	^{1}/$_{2}$lb
280g		9oz	
315g		10oz	
345g		11oz	
375g		12oz	^{3}/$_{4}$lb
410g		13oz	
440g		14oz	
470g		15oz	
1000g	1kg	35.2oz	2.2lb
	1.5kg		3.3lb

Oven temperatures

The Celsius temperatures given here are not exact; they have been rounded off and are given as a guide only. Follow the manufacturer's temperature guide, relating it to oven description given in the recipe. Remember gas ovens are hottest at the top, electric ovens at the bottom and convection-fan forced ovens are usually even throughout. We included Regulo numbers for gas cookers which may assist. To convert °C to °F multiply °C by 9 and divide by 5 then add 32.

Oven temperatures

	C°	F°	Regulo
Very slow	120	250	1
Slow	150	300	2
Moderately slow	150	325	3
Moderate	180	350	4
Moderately hot	190-200	370-400	5-6
Hot	210-220	410-440	6-7
Very hot	230	450	8
Super hot	250-290	475-500	9-10

Cake dish sizes

Metric	Imperial
15cm	6in
18cm	7in
20cm	8in
23cm	9in

Loaf dish sizes

Metric	Imperial
23x12cm	9x5in
25x8cm	10x3in
28x18cm	11x7in

Liquid measures

Metric	Imperial	Cup & Spoon
mL	fl oz	
millilitres	fluid ounce	
5ml	$^1/_6$fl oz	1 teaspoon
20ml	$^2/_3$fl oz	1 tablespoon
30ml	1fl oz	1 tablespoon plus 2 teaspoons
60ml	2fl oz	$^1/_4$ cup
85ml	2$^1/_2$fl oz	$^1/_3$ cup
100ml	3fl oz	$^3/_8$ cup
125ml	4fl oz	$^1/_2$ cup
150ml	5fl oz	$^1/_4$ pint, 1 gill
250ml	8fl oz	1 cup
300ml	10fl oz	$^1/_2$ pint)
360ml	12fl oz	1$^1/_2$ cups
420ml	14fl oz	1$^3/_4$ cups
500ml	16fl oz	2 cups
600ml	20fl oz 1 pint,	2$^1/_2$ cups
1 litre	35fl oz 1 $^3/_4$ pints,	4 cups

Cup measurements

One cup is equal to the following weights.

	Metric	Imperial
Almonds, flaked	90g	3oz
Almonds, slivered, ground	125g	4oz
Almonds, kernel	155g	5oz
Apples, dried, chopped	125g	4oz
Apricots, dried, chopped	190g	6oz
Breadcrumbs, packet	125g	4oz

	Metric	Imperial
Breadcrumbs, soft	60g	2oz
Cheese, grated	125g	4oz
Choc bits	155g	5oz
Coconut, desiccated	90g	3oz
Cornflakes	30g	1oz
Currants	155g	5oz
Flour	125g	4oz
Fruit, dried (mixed, sultanas etc)	185g	6oz
Ginger, crystallised, glace	250g	8oz
Honey, treacle, golden syrup	315g	10oz
Mixed peel	220g	7oz
Nuts, chopped	125g	4oz
Prunes, chopped	220g	7oz
Rice, cooked	155g	5oz
Rice, uncooked	220g	7oz
Rolled oats	90g	3oz
Sesame seeds	125g	4oz
Shortening (butter, margarine)	250g	8oz
Sugar, brown	155g	5oz
Sugar, granulated or caster	250g	8oz
Sugar, sifted icing	155g	5oz
Wheatgerm	60g	2oz

Length

Some of us are still having trouble converting imperial to metric. In this scale, measures have been rounded off to the easiest-to-use and most acceptable figures.

To obtain the exact metric equivalent to convert inches to centimetres, multiply inches by 2.54 Therefore 1 inch equals 25.4 millimetres and 1 millimetre equals 0.03937 inches.

Metric	Imperial
mm = millimetres	in = inches
cm = centimetres	ft = feet
5mm, 0.5cm	$^1/_4$in
10mm, 1.0cm	$^1/_2$in
20mm, 2.0cm	$^3/_4$in
2.5cm	1in
5cm	2in
8cm	3in
10cm	4in
12cm	5in
15cm	6in
18cm	7in
20cm	8in
23cm	9in
25cm	10in
28cm	11in
30cm	1 ft, 12in

index